BIG ICK ENERGY

A SELECTION OF THE WORLD'S WEIRDEST TURN-OFFS

summersdale

An Hachette UK Company
www.hachette.co.uk

Summersdale Publishers
Part of Octopus Publishing Group Limited
Carmelite House
50 Victoria Embankment
LONDON
EC4Y 0DZ
UK

www.summersdale.com

Printed and bound in Poland

ISBN: 978-1-83799-523-3

This FSC® label means that materials used for the product have been responsibly sourced

MIX
Paper | Supporting responsible forestry
FSC® C018236

Substantial discounts on bulk quantities of Summersdale books are available to corporations, professional associations and other organizations. For details contact general enquiries: telephone: +44 (0) 1243 771107 or email: enquiries@summersdale.com.

To ....

From ....

INTRODUCTION

Do you cringe when you hear someone giving a ridiculously overcomplicated coffee order? Do you shudder when someone sits the wrong way round on a chair? Do you die inside when you see a person running somewhere while wearing a backpack?

In the bustling chaos of our everyday lives, we often encounter those tiny, cringe-worthy moments that make us squirm. Fear not. *Big Ick Energy* invites you to revel in the delightful immorality of passing unfounded judgments on the unsuspecting individuals who cross your path. So, dive into these pages and embrace the liberating joy of casting whimsical critiques with abandon!

Chasing after a
ping-pong ball.

Walking back
after their turn
at bowling.

KNEE-LENGTH JEAN SHORTS.

WEARING FLIP-FLOPS IN A NON-FLIP-FLOP-APPROPRIATE SITUATION.

Having an
Instagram account
for their pet.

WEARING
SUNGLASSES
INDOORS.

PICKING SOMETHING UP WITH THEIR FEET.

WHEN THEY HAVE A PODCAST.

Texting a radio station
and asking them to
"keep the tunes coming".

CHEWING LOUDLY.

FAILING TO CATCH A BALL.

Having long toenails.

Wearing shoes
without socks.

Any use of corporate
jargon, especially
in normal life.

WHEN THEY
WAVE ON ZOOM
MEETINGS.

The little run they
do when someone
is holding the
door open.

Taking an age to pack their items at the self-checkout and holding up the queue.

BRUSHING THEIR HAIR IN PUBLIC.

SEEING THEM WALK,
DRIPPING WET,
FROM THE POOL
TO THEIR TOWEL.

JOGGING IN PLACE
AT A ROAD CROSSING.

Wearing
washing-up
gloves.

**BRIGHTLY
COLOURED
SKINNY JEANS.**

WEARING
SOCKS IN BED.

Talking loudly
on the phone on
public transport.

When they
push a pull.

When they
pull a push.

WHEN THEIR UMBRELLA TURNS INSIDE OUT.

Seeing them walk down the middle of the train to find a seat.

When they get
the lyrics wrong but
believe they're right.

BITS OF FOOD
STUCK IN
THEIR TEETH.

THE PHRASE
"GOING FORWARD".

BASEBALL CAPS
WORN THE WRONG
WAY ROUND.

When they
stick their tongue
out while writing.

**NOT GIVING
A TIP.**

EATING WITH
THEIR CUTLERY
HELD IN
BALLED FISTS.

Dressing gowns.

When people who
can't rap, rap.

Walking up to
an automatic door
that won't open.

AVIATORS.

Being the first
person on the
dance floor.

WHEN THEY PLAY MINI GOLF AND THEY'RE TOO TALL FOR THE CLUB.

BEING STRAPPED INTO A RIDE AT THE THEME PARK.

Wiping their dusty or greasy fingers on their trousers after eating.

WHEN THEIR PERFUME OR AFTERSHAVE IS TOO STRONG.

When they have to wear the little bib at the hairdressers.

SEXY DANCE TRENDS ON SOCIAL MEDIA.

ADDRESSING STRANGERS AS "LOVE" OR "BABE".

Casually singing but trying to make it sound good.

Overcomplicated
drinks orders.

When they mistakenly
think someone is smiling
or waving at them.

LOUD,
WET KISSING.

Having bulging
pockets because
there's too much
stuff in them.

People who refer to their friend or partner as "this one" in a social media post.

When they shout, "Lads, lads, lads!"

PEOPLE WHO
MICROWAVE FISH.

BRIEFCASE USERS.

Biting the fork
when they eat.

CLAPPING WHEN
THE PLANE LANDS.

WHEN THEY DON'T PUT THEIR SHOES ON PROPERLY AND CRUSH THE BACKS WHILE THEY WALK.

Winking.

When they're the first person to sing the slow "Haaa" of "Happy Birthday".

Biting off tiny bits of remaining apple from the core.

ROAD RAGE.

When they use a
stylus for their
touchscreen.

WHEN THEY LAUGH LONGER THAN NECESSARY AT SOMETHING THAT IS ONLY MILDLY FUNNY.

When they hobble barefoot across stones on the beach.

COFFEE BREATH.

SITTING THE WRONG WAY ROUND ON A CHAIR.

Mansplaining.

MANSPREADING.

HAVING
THEMSELVES AS
THEIR PHONE
BACKGROUND.

High-fiving
after sex.

Not being able
to whisk properly.

Being the first to
arrive at a social event.

STALLING A CAR.

Not being able
to make up their
mind when
ordering food.

Offering a comment rather than a question when someone says, "Any questions?"

Asking a long-winded question when someone says, "Any questions?"

People who touch
their mouth and nose
a lot when they talk.

NOVELTY TIES.

*DANCING
SLIGHTLY
OFFBEAT.*

**PEOPLE WHO
KISS THEIR PETS
ON THE MOUTH.**

WHEN THEY
PUT ON A
BABY VOICE.

The
where-are-my-keys
pat down.

Weak handshakes.

Clammy handshakes.

WEARING A
WOOLLY HAT
INDOORS.

Scrunching their
toes up weirdly
because the
floor is cold.

DRINKING STRAIGHT OUT OF A CARTON IN A SHARED HOUSEHOLD.

People who say, "One more sleep."

MISMATCHED
SOCKS.

USING THEIR INDEX
FINGER TO SCROLL
ON THEIR PHONE.

When someone bends over and puts their foot on a ledge to tie their shoelace.

SEEING THEM BUY TOILET ROLL.

USING
CONTROLLERS
WITH GREASY
FINGERS.

People who talk
about themselves in
the third person.

Using "boo" as an affectionate term.

Bare feet on the coffee table.

ADULTS WHO REFER
TO THEIR PARENTS
AS "MUMMY"
OR "DADDY".

People who refer
to themselves
as their pet's
"mummy" or "daddy".

Lip-sync
TikToks.

SUCKING
EACH FINGER
AFTER EATING
SOMETHING.

WATCHING THEM
PULL THE PITH
OFF ORANGES.

DRINKING PLAIN
BOILED WATER.

When they run
for a bus or train.

PEOPLE WHO
REFER TO
"THE INTERWEB".

WATCHING THEM WAIT FOR A RECEIPT.

People who use a fishing photo on their dating profile.

Sitting on
the bed in
outdoor clothes.

Sitting on the bed
with shoes on.

MINI
BEANIE HATS.

Watching them
struggle to eat
peanut butter
without smacking
their lips.

When people put their hands on their hips and slip their fingers under the waistband of their trousers.

SCRAPING PLATES AND BOWLS WHEN EATING.

HACKING UP
PHLEGM.

LEG JIGGLERS.

Little concentration
noises when
they're working.

**PEOPLE WHO GO
TO MUSIC SHOPS
SPECIFICALLY TO
PLAY THE PIANOS
FOR ATTENTION.**

DRINKING
BOTTLED WATER
AT HOME.

Walking slowly.

People who pretend to have less money than they actually do.

Audible tea and coffee gulping.

WHEN THEY HAVE TO LOOK UP HOW TO TIE A TIE ON YOUTUBE.

People who do the finger wiggle when selecting a chocolate from the box.

Typing on a keyboard really loudly in a public place.

WHEN THEY READ WITH THEIR FINGER FOLLOWING THE LINE.

SEEING SOMEONE
SIT IN THE BACK OF
A SMALL CAR.

SWIMMING
GOGGLES.

People who use takeaway coffee as an accessory.

UN-IRONIC USE OF "YOLO".

Barefoot shoes.

WHEN THEY HAVE
TO OPEN THEIR
CAR DOOR TO
CHECK WHETHER
THEY'RE IN THE
PARKING SPACE.

When they grasp
the mixing spoon
with their fist and
stir like a child.

**FAKE
HOUSEPLANTS.**

COOKIE DUNKING.

Watching someone drink the soggy cookie-crumb tea at the bottom of the cup.

WHEN THEY TRY
TO PRONOUNCE
MENU ITEMS WITH
AN ACCENT.

People who
eat spaghetti with
a knife and fork.

WHEN THEY SAY THEY'RE "NOT LIKE OTHER GIRLS/GUYS".

WATCHING SOMEONE RUN UP THE STAIRS ON ALL FOURS.

Sitting in the bath.

WATCHING SOMEONE HAVE "HAPPY BIRTHDAY" SUNG TO THEM.

WHEN THEY THINK THAT NOT HOLDING ON ON PUBLIC TRANSPORT MAKES THEM LOOK COOL.

When they lose their balance on public transport.

Saying "I'll do..."
instead of "I'll have..."
or "I would like..."
when ordering food.

Falling over.

RUNNING WITH
A BACKPACK ON.

People who
overshare on
social media.

Referring to the football team that they support as "we".

TYPING ON A KEYBOARD WITH TWO FINGERS.

WHEN THEY REFER
TO THEMSELVES AS
AN "ALPHA MALE"
OR "BOSS BABE".

FANNY PACKS.

People who undo the zip on their trousers on the way to the bathroom.

PEOPLE WHO EXIT A BATHROOM DOING UP THE ZIP OF THEIR TROUSERS.

"LIVE, LAUGH, LOVE" DÉCOR.

Having a laptop actually on their lap.

PEOPLE WHO SET REAL MUSIC AS THEIR RINGTONE.

When they ask for a straw for their drink.

PEOPLE WHO BREAK
THE SPAGHETTI
IN HALF BEFORE
THEY COOK IT.

Doing a performative
birthday social media
post for someone else
and posting loads of
pictures of themselves.

People who use "Feeding time at the zoo" as a caption on videos of friends and family dining.

FANCY FONTS ON THEIR SOCIAL MEDIA BIO.

PEOPLE WHO PLAY AIR GUITAR TO A SONG.

PEOPLE WHO AIR DRUM TO A SONG.

Overexaggerated shows of satisfaction when taking the first bite of food.

WHEN THEY HAVE TO CHASE AFTER SOMETHING THAT'S CAUGHT IN THE WIND.

PEOPLE WHO CLICK THEIR FINGERS AT THE WAITER.

The "Can I have the bill?" air gesture.

Grown adults whining.

PEOPLE WHO
WIPE SAUCE OFF
THEIR PLATE WITH
THEIR FINGER.

PEOPLE WHO RUN WITH THEIR HEAD THRUST FORWARD.

When they repeatedly stumble but neither catch their balance nor fall so the stumbling looks like a flailing dance.

WHEN SOMEONE IS TOO OBVIOUSLY WAITING FOR LAUGHTER AFTER MAKING A JOKE.

When they watch TV with their mouth open.

PEOPLE WHO DO A LITTLE ROCK BACK AND FORTH ON THEIR HEELS WHEN TALKING BUSINESS.

WATCHING THEM USE CLINGFILM.

Blowing on their food to cool it down.

PUTTING FOOD IN THEIR MOUTH AND *THEN* BLOWING TO COOL IT DOWN USING THE OPEN-MOUTHED "HAFASHAHSAHSHFAH" TECHNIQUE.

HOLDING OUT
THEIR CARD
BEFORE THE
CARD MACHINE
IS READY.

When they're
spun around in the
hairdresser's chair for
the "grand reveal".

BUYING SOMETHING FROM A VENDING MACHINE.

People who bite their nails.

WATCHING
THEM BLOW OUT
THEIR BIRTHDAY
CANDLES.

When they're really
thirsty and drink a
whole glass of water
while breathing heavily
through their nose.

WHEN THEY SUCK CHOCOLATE BARS INSTEAD OF CHEWING THEM LIKE A NORMAL PERSON.

WHEN THEY TAKE THEIR SOCKS OFF LAST.

PEOPLE WHO COUNT ON THEIR FINGERS.

Seeing someone sitting in their car when they stop at traffic lights.

SAYING "AHHH"
AFTER TAKING
A SIP OF TEA.

Referring to a child's
age in months after
they're three years old.

USING ACRONYMS
IN EVERYDAY
SPEECH.

When they walk
downhill and their
feet slap on the floor.

When they do
a little jump to
pull up their jeans.

When they look at
something up close and
you see their eyes cross.

People who
double-dip.

PEOPLE WHO POST
A PHOTO OF A
GLASS OF WINE ON
SOCIAL MEDIA WITH
A CAPTION THAT
SUGGESTS IT'S
A DARING AND
ORIGINAL ACTIVITY.

DOING A VICTORY
AIR PUNCH IN A
BUSINESS SETTING.

Being a sore
loser as an adult.

FLOSSING (TEETH) IN PUBLIC.

FLOSSING (DANCE) IN PUBLIC.

Tying their shoes with the bunny ears method.

WHEN THEY SMELL FOOD BEFORE EATING IT AND YOU SEE THEIR NOSTRILS FLARE.

WHEN THEY DRINK
TOO FAST AND
WATER SPILLS
OVER THE SIDE OF
THEIR MOUTH.

People who
make loud grunting
noises at the gym.

Playing loud music on a speaker in public.

When you see them standing in a queue.

"READJUSTING"
IN PUBLIC.

People who post
pictures of themselves
on social media with
the caption, "Felt cute,
might delete later."

When they look at the waiter eagerly, only to realize it isn't their food as they pass by the table.

WATCHING THEM FURIOUSLY SCRATCH AN ITCH.

SINGING "HAPPY BIRTHDAY" AND TRYING TO MAKE IT SOUND GOOD.

WHEN THEY WATCH THEIR OWN INSTAGRAM STORY.

People who stop to check their phone halfway through a conversation.

ROLLER SKATING OR ICE SKATING BADLY.

People who make tea in stained mugs.

WATCHING THEM HESITANTLY DIP THEIR TOE IN THE BATH OR POOL TO CHECK THE TEMPERATURE.

When you can hear them peeing through the bathroom door.

When you hear anything else through the bathroom door...

KNUCKLE CRACKS.

**BALANCING ON
A BIKE WHEN IT'S
STATIONARY.**

People who intentionally eat with their mouth open because, "Air circulating the palate improves the flavour."

HICCUPS.

COUNTING OUT
CHANGE.

WALKING SLOWLY
WITH FULL BEER
GLASSES AND
STRUGGLING NOT
TO SPILL THEM.

People who keep a
tissue up their sleeve
and return it there after
blowing their nose.

**WHEN YOU
SEE THEIR LEGS
UNDERWATER.**

WHEN THEY WEAR
THEIR BACKPACK
TOO HIGH ON
THEIR BACK.

When they don't
like vegetables
as an adult.

WHEN YOU'RE FILLING UP THE CAR WITH FUEL AND THEY LOOK UP AT YOU THROUGH THE PASSENGER WINDOW.

When they shout, "Shots, shots, shots!"

MOIST MOUTH NOISES.

People who repeatedly press the backspace button instead of selecting the text and hitting the delete button once.

When they smell
their clothes to
check the freshness.

IMAGINING
THEM AT WORK.

WATCHING THEM ADDRESS AN ENVELOPE.

LICKING A STAMP.

Using the term
"levelling up"
anywhere, anytime.

**BEING VISIBLY
EMBARRASSED.**

WHEN THEY THINK
THEY'VE LOST YOU
IN A BUSY PLACE
AND YOU SEE THEM
LOOKING AROUND
LIKE A LOST DOG.

When they
call themselves
a "girlie".

WHEN THEY TIP THE CRUMBS FROM A PACKET INTO THEIR MOUTH BUT MISS.

Taking karaoke too seriously.

SITTING CROSS-LEGGED.

People who refer to celebrities by their first name in conversation, as if they are friends with them.

Anyone who leans back and pats their tummy after eating a big meal.

WHEN THEY ACCIDENTALLY BANG THEIR HEAD.

WHEN PEOPLE FOLD
THE CORNER OF A
BOOK OR MAGAZINE
PAGE DOWN.

PEOPLE WHO SPIT
WHEN THEY TALK.

When they can't
handle spice.

**USING WACKY
FILTERS ON
ZOOM CALLS.**

Cycling Lycra.

WHEN YOU'RE WATCHING A MOVIE AND THEY KEEP INTERRUPTING TO TELL YOU WHERE THEY'VE SEEN THE ACTORS BEFORE.

When one of their feet sticks out of the covers.

Having a lunchbox.

MIRROR SELFIES.

Checking themselves out while walking past a shop window.

BUYING THE PHOTOS YOU GET FROM ROLLERCOASTER RIDES.

When they spit out toothpaste.

PEOPLE WHO INSIST ON TASTING WINE BEFORE IT'S SERVED IN A RESTAURANT.

SWINGING ON A SWING.

When they park at the far end of a car park.

SAYING "SUPER COOL".

PERSONALIZED NUMBER PLATES.

Crossing the road.

Having to walk
out of the shallow
bit of the sea.

Watching them
eat a lollipop.

SITTING ON
A CHAIR THAT'S
TOO SMALL.

Sitting on a chair
that's too high.

PUTTING THEIR CARD ON THE WRONG PART OF THE CONTACTLESS PAYMENT MACHINE.

Overusing the words "literally" and "like".

WHEN PEOPLE HAVE DRIPPY HANDS AFTER NOT DRYING THEM COMPLETELY.

WALKING ON TIPTOE.

When people
comment on celebrities'
Instagram posts.

PEOPLE WHO REFER
TO THE COVID-19
PANDEMIC AS
"THE PANNY D".

WATCHING THEM
GET DOWN OFF
THE TOP BUNK.

Seeing them
wearing any kind
of safety harness.

Watching them struggle to eat something too big for their mouth.

When they strap their bike helmet on.

NOT BEING ABLE TO PARK.

WHEN A DRIBBLE OF MELTED ICE CREAM RUNS ON TO THEIR HAND BECAUSE THEY DIDN'T LICK EVENLY AROUND THE TOP OF THE CONE.

Walking around
with a paper map.

GOING DOWN
A SLIDE.

STRUGGLING TO PUT A SHEET ON A BED.

Short-sleeved button-up shirts (especially when worn with a tie).

Crouching for a photo when there is no need to crouch for the photo.

WHEN THEY TRY TO HOLD A PET BUT IT SCRAMBLES OUT OF THEIR ARMS.

NOT KNOWING
HOW TO HOLD
A BABY.

Being led on a horse.

Using any kind
of filter on a
social media post.

When they're super
into cryptocurrency.

PUTTING ALL OF
THEIR HOLIDAY
PHOTOS ON
FACEBOOK.

Not being
able to pour a
beer properly.

SEEING THEM WAIT WHILE CHEESE OR PEPPER IS SPRINKLED ON THEIR MEAL AT A RESTAURANT.

Being bad at DIY.

SOCKS THAT ONLY COVER THEIR TOES.

WHEN THEY BALANCE A PLATE ON THEIR KNEES TO EAT.

WEARING AN APRON.

When they pose for a photo and put their hand on the other person's stomach.

NOT KNOWING
HOW TO SHARE
THEIR SCREEN ON
A ZOOM CALL.

When their butt
crack is showing.

Hunching
over to eat.

When people
refer to amateur
photoshoots as "shoots".

WHEN THEY MAKE SOCIAL MEDIA POSTS ABOUT THEIR "ICKS".

THE LITTLE BOOK OF FLIRTING

SADIE CAYMAN

PAPERBACK

978-1-83799-080-1

Packed with essential advice for everyone from flirting first-timers to anyone looking for some fresh dating inspiration

Whether you choose to treat your flirting talents as a delicate science or simply as a fun way to meet new people, this pocket guide will set you well on your way to charming the socks off anyone you set your sights on.

From chat-up lines and online-dating nopes to first-date ideas and etiquette, these pages will arm you with all the flirting know-how you could ever need.

THE LITTLE BOOK OF FARTS

HARDBACK

978-1-83799-278-2

If you thought there was only one type of fart, get ready to be blown away!

This amusing and informative little book is set to entertain farters far and wide. Featuring all things flatulence, it's the perfect gift for toilet-humoured-trouser-coughers!

Human beings are made unique by a selection of special and beautiful things: our fingerprints, our irises, our voices... and our farts.

Covering the many different types of farts, farty facts (did you know, a person farts around 15 times a day?), farting etiquette, top-trumping tips and bottom-burp analysis, this book is sure to make you laugh out loud and let one rip.

Have you enjoyed this book?

If so, find us on Facebook
at Summersdale Publishers,
on Twitter/X at @Summersdale
and on Instagram and TikTok at
@summersdalebooks and get in
touch. We'd love to hear from you!

www.summersdale.com